REAL
PUNCHING

GEOFF THOMPSON 4th DAN
JOINT CHIEF INSTRUCTOR C.E.K.A.

JOINT CHIEF INSTRUCTOR
BRITISH COMBAT ASSOCIATION

ABOUT THE AUTHOR

GEOFF THOMPSON WAS A DOORMAN FOR NINE YEARS AND HAS BEEN A PRACTISING MARTIAL ARTIST FOR OVER TWENTY. HE IS PRESENTLY QUALIFIED AS AN A.B.A.ASS. BOXING COACH, BRITISH AMATEUR WRESTLING ASSOCIATION COACH AND HOLDS A 4th DAN C.E.K.A., 4th DAN B.C.A., 2nd DAN K.U.G.B., AND 1st DAN MODGA KUNG FU. GEOFF IS A FORMER BRITISH WEAPONS CHAMPION, HAS COMPETED IN THE U.S.A. AND HAS ALSO TRAINED WIDELY IN AIKIDO, JUDO AND IS QUALIFIED TO TEACH JU-JITSU.

GEOFF'S FIRST BOOK **WATCH MY BACK -** *A BOUNCER'S STORY* IS FAST BECOMING A CULT BOOK. HIS SECOND AND THIRD BOOKS, **THE PAVEMENT ARENA** AND **REAL SELF DEFENCE** HAVE ALSO BEEN WIDELY ACCLAIMED. HE NOW WRITES REGULAR COLUMNS FOR COMBAT MAGAZINE, TRADITIONAL KARATE MAGAZINE AND MUSCLE MAG. HE IS WIDELY RECOGNISED AS AN INTERNATIONAL AUTHORITY ON THE ART OF SELF PROTECTION.

FOR A GREATER INSIGHT INTO THE ARTS OF GRAPPLING AND KICKING PLEASE REFER TO GEOFF'S BOOKS **REAL GRAPPLING** AND **REAL KICKING**.

ACKNOWLEDGEMENTS

Thanks to **Dennis Young** for all his patient instruction in the many splendoured world of western boxing, to **Clive MacIntosh**, and to my very good friend **Tom Sharp.**

ALSO MY GOOD FRIEND AND PARTNER IN THE BRITISH COMBAT ASSOCIATION, **PETER CONSTERDINE** FOR HIS CONTINUED SUPPORT.

TO MY BEAUTIFUL SHARON

By the same author -

Watch My Back
- A Bouncer's Story

The Pavement Arena
- Adapting Combat Martial Arts to the Street

Real Self Defence

Real Grappling

Real Kicking

Bouncer; (sequal to Watch My Back)

Summersdale Publishers
PO Box 49
Chichester
West Sussex
PO19 4LF
United Kingdom

A CIP catalogue record for this book is available from the British Library.

Printed and bound in Great Britain by The Book Factory, London.

ISBN 1 873475 26 8

CONTENTS

PROLOGUE

A carpenter is knowledgeable about working with wood, a painter is knowledgeable about working with paint, and a pugilist who has mastered his craft should be knowledgeable about thre mechanics of punching!

The importance of correct punching is that it is an art like any other art that must be practised to be perfected. It is about repetitive work, done over and over again with sound knowledge of the correct techniques.

'To kill a cockroach' is a term used in New York boxing gyms by coaches to fighters practising the execution of a pile driving left hook done to maximum effect with a swivel of the left foot/ankle as if you were crushing a cockroach with your foot, hence the catchphrase, transferring the body weight from left foot to right foot.

The fundamentals and techniques vary for the vast arsenal of different punches in a gladiator/pugilist's repertoire. To maximise all the varying punches to their maximum effect the warrior must have the mentality and mental strength and courage of his convictions to be whole-heartedly 100% committed to his cause, because in the words of Sugar Ray Leonard, top level fighting/combat is 80% mental!

Jim McDonnell

British & Europrean Professional Boxing Champion
Boxing Commentator for Sky Television

INTRODUCTION

WHY PUNCHING?

Having had to face several hundred opponents 'in the street' and having been witness to thousands of 'live' fights over the last ten years I have come to the conclusion that a 'real' exponent of the fighting arts must incorporate all distances in his fighting discipline, after all a chain is only as strong as its weakest link. The distance that most systems seem to favour is kicking distance, this is probably due to its attractiveness or perhaps 'celluloid peer pressure' (see my book **Real Kicking**) the most neglected distance of course is the devastating art of grappling (see my book **Real Grappling**) due to its Martial ugliness.

In between these two distances is punching, a seemingly indifferent range, not neglected though neither noticed. When you consider that most street confrontations start with some kind of dialogue, (see my book **Real Self Defence**) usually occurring at 'Punching range' it makes you wonder why, if punching range is the distance given, so many want to manufacture another, stepping out for a kick or in for a throw, ignoring that which is so startlingly immediate. It is simply a matter of logic that the closest and most available tool to the target is the very one to use. In nine out of ten cases the most available tool will be the hands. As demonstrated in **Real Grappling**, wrestling is a support art and as demonstrated in **Real Kicking**, kicking is, also a support art, punching, as I hope to demonstrate in this volume is THE MAIN ARTILLERY, the first line of attack.

For those interested in the art of pugilism this book also takes into account the sporting aspect.

Take a look on the sports shelf of any book shop and you will find a myriad of books on and about various fighting systems of the world, all encompassing the theories and technique of the ryu therein. This book differs from the foregoing in three ways; One; It isolates the 'hands' as attacking tools. Two; The techniques herein, though predominantly western boxing, may be utilised in, and are indeed born from, every system, and Three; All of the techniques endorsed in this text are empirical.

Most fighting systems of the world are uncannily similar. All offer the lead hand punch, reverse punch, hooks and uppercuts. The defences against the same are, also very alike. In my opinion it is the western boxing system of pugilism that rises above the maelstrom of other systems when 'advanced' punching is called for, this statement is not meant as a bias nor is it intended to offend, it's just an honest opinion based on years of pressure testing in the field.

The fact that the western boxer is ill prepared for both kicking and grappling ranges is out of the context of this book. This text may become the 'missing piece' in the martial arts jigsaw and will complete what was otherwise an unfinished picture.

If you are not that familiar with punching you may well wonder what more there is to be said about the subject, after all, a punch is just a punch, or so it would appear. The reason why I wrote this book and why it has found shelf space within the book shops is that a punch is far more than just a punch. A deeper look will unveil a labyrinth of concealed knowledge, an Aladdin's cave of intricacies and a treasure trove of 'data' that will enable the neophyte to punch and the expert to punch better.

'Hands' are the most accessible, effective and natural tool available for utilisation and survival on the 'pavement Arena'. Conscientious adherence to the techniques and theory's herein will not only improve/perfect your punching ability for the dojo/gym it will also help markedly in your search for survival in a society cruelly infected with the disease 'VIOLENCE!' This book, as with all my books, is empirical, all of its techniques 'pressure tested' in an arena unshackled by rules, regulations, whistles and bells, where one mistake may prove fatal. I have successfully employed all of the techniques here endorsed 'in the field'. (I spend a lot of time in fields, don't I?)

With this in mind excellence in punching technique should be readily sought, and as quickly as possible, after all, you never never know how soon you may need their services.

CHAPTER ONE

BODY MECHANICS

Before I segregate and dissect the various compartments of 'over all' punching I would like to take a look at body mechanics, the practice of body weight transference, after all, it is from here that 'power' is derived. The fist is only the implement that delivers the blow, the 'bullet' if you like. The body, or the gun, is the power source, the generator, or the engine. Punching without body sponsorship will relegate your blows to the realms of ineffectiveness. Paradoxically the puncher who does utilise full body weight transference when executing a punch will amass tremendous power. A 9 stone fighter in a street scenario who 'punches his weight' with accuracy will find no difficulty knocking unconscious an 18 stone adversary.

Body mechanics is a system where by one drives the body weight, via the hip (and the hara) behind a chosen punch. Many practitioners, especially heavier people, punch from the arm or the shoulder utilising only a small part of the body weight, this may still generate a small percentage of available power but it will be minimal. To produce maximum power one must punch from the stomach, some call this focal point the 'Hara' and hint of internal power, though more realistically the 'Hara' (to be found in the belly button area of the abdomen) is the body's centre of gravity, to punch from here enables you to utilise the entire body weight, down to the ounce.

In theory this appears simple, the hip (left side or right side, depending upon which arm you employ to punch) follows the path of the elected punch. A right cross sees the right side of the hip (from an orthodox stance) travelling forward along the same route as the punch, a left hook sees the left side of the hip (from an orthodox stance) travelling behind and along the same route as the punch. In the relevant chapters on individual punches I shall digress more.

In practice, of course, this is not quite as easy as it sounds, it requires great skill which is only born from much practice and perseverance. Like a finely tuned engine every thing must work in conjunction if smooth running is to be attained and maintained, if one small particle is out of 'sync' with the rest, smooth running will be lost. If the hip travels through too soon, power is lost, too late, power is lost, if the hip is not fully extended, power is again lost, if the hip is over extended, balance is impaired, if you over concentrate on hip commitment you may under-concentrate on other important factors like targeting, if the punch is off target all is wasted any way. Add to this list 'Kime' (body focus) and you have one more factor to consider. Every system, consciously or subconsciously, employs 'Kime' though they may not label it as so.

Kime is a means of focusing (or tensing) the body on the moment of impact, (the attacks impact upon the target) the muscles collectively 'tense' for a split second when your punch connects with the target, adding markedly to the power input of the said strike.

Kime must also run in conjunction with the hip thrust. Kime too soon or too late and its input is greatly or completely lost.

For the blow to maximise kime and hip thrust must culminate at the exact instance when the punch connects with the target, if they do not and are out of sync then you will be out of 'luck'. Once the three factors are running nicely in conjunction and power has been attained you will (should) be 'punching your weight'. For those who strive for more (greedy) there is another advancement, 'Travelling' (this doesn't mean punching some one on the train) 'Travelling' with a technique is an advanced concept. In the 'crawl', 'walk' and 'run' syndrome travelling is the 'sprint'. To 'Travel' is to add to all of the foregoing criteria a step or a shuffle along the same route as the punch adding the momentum of moving body weight to hip thrust and kime.

For instance, from orthodox stance, when throwing a right cross you would step or shuffle forward with your left lead leg followed directly by your reverse right leg, this would be employed in conjunction with the hip thrust and kime. Theoretically it sounds easy, in practice it is not so. A step too close or not close enough to the target will put your distancing out, forcing the punch to lose power due to its over close proximity to the target, or miss the target completely because it is not close enough. If your 'step' before or after the punch the generated forward momentum will be lost and the 'travel' wasted, if the 'step' is too slow it will 'telegraph' your chosen punch. The extra power gained by travelling is amassed from the forward momentum of your body weight, to harness this power completely your forward moving leg and thus the body weight, should land in time with the impact of the blow or still be moving forward as the punch strikes the target, indeed a difficult task, but, with much practice it is easily attainable.

Putting it down on paper makes it all seem rather complicated, don't be discouraged by this veil because once lifted it will all seem rather simple, as Bruce Lee said, and I quote,

"BEFORE I STARTED TRAINING IN THE MARTIAL ARTS A PUNCH WAS JUST A PUNCH, A KICK JUST A KICK, WHEN I STARTED, A PUNCH WAS NO LONGER JUST A PUNCH, A KICK NO LONGER JUST A KICK. NOW THAT I UNDERSTAND TRAINING A PUNCH IS, AGAIN, JUST A PUNCH, A KICK JUST A KICK."

CHAPTER TWO

STANCES

Choosing a stance is important, a bad posture will relegate your punching to lacklustre.

There are only two stances that are worthy of contention when it comes to choice, orthodox stance (left leg leading) and southpaw stance (right leg leading). As a general rule of thumb the orthodox stance is employed by the right handed fighter, the southpaw stance by the left handed fighter. Both former and latter leave the strongest hand at the rear, a little like chess where the weaker pawns lead the board and protect the stronger ruck, king and queen at the back.

This is my recommended system of use.

If you are left handed and opt for the southpaw stance please reverse the forthcoming instructions which are based on the orthodox fighter.

ORTHODOX STANCE; Left leg leading with the left foot turned slightly inwards, toes gripping the floor to enhance balance and stability. Rear right foot turned inwards on the ball of the foot (see illus.) to enhance speed of movement and aid hip twist. Legs shoulder width apart at a 45 degree angle (this angle offers ultimate balance and stability and should be maintained at all times).

Both knees should be bent. from the hip upwards the torso should be turned at a 45 degree angle to narrow the opponent's target area, thus protecting the vulnerable solo plexus (under the breast bone).

Both elbows should be kept tightly in to the body to protect the abdomen/ribs/kidneys etc.

Right and left fists should be situated at each side of the jaw for its protection.

The head should be tilted with the chin touching the chest, forcing you to roll the eyes upward to see straight, this will protect the highly vulnerable chin/jaw. Hunching up the shoulders also adds to its protection.

Keep the fists relaxed with both palms facing inwards. If the fists are constantly flexed energy will be expended needlessly, only tense the fists on impact with the target.

Southpaw stance is a direct facsimile to orthodox stance with the right leg leading as opposed to the left.

Maintenance of the stance through out a fight is imperative, an off balance fighter will be easily knocked over or out.

The advanced player may move the arms from the conventional guard position other than to execute a punch but care should be taken not to leave the jaw exposed.

If you drop either side of the guard, for what ever reason, bring the shoulder of the relaxed arm up and above the chin line (see illus) as a back up guard. Never drop both arms at the same time, always leave at least one arm protecting the jaw.

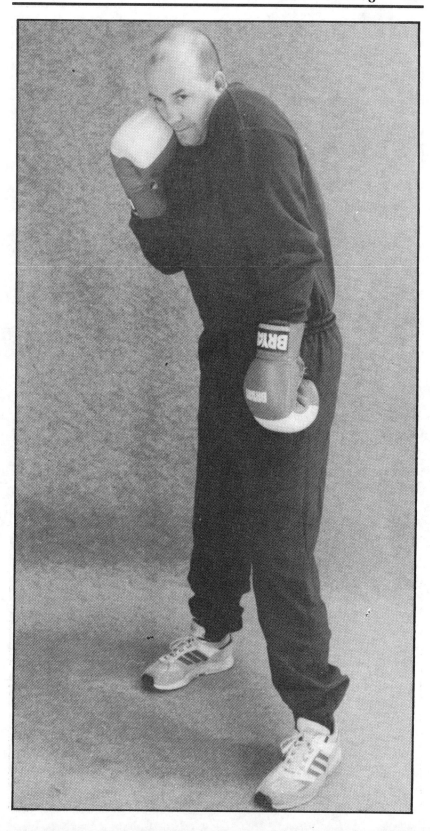

CHAPTER THREE

THE JAB

A very underrated punch, often seen as being a weak, support punch to the more consequential cross or hook. In reality it is a multifarious, potentially powerful, blow that is the fundamental driving force of all other punches.

Traditionally we see the jab performed in three ways that vary very little in style or stature.

KARATE;

The Karataka throws the jab, or lead hand punch, from a low guard or from the hip position (hikatae), twisting the fist and torso on impact with the target, the right supporting hand being sharply retracted to the opposite hip thus leaving the upper torso and face of the puncher, exposed Even at an advanced level 'hikatae' is encouraged.

KUNG-FU;

The kung-fu practitioner operates in a similar genre to the Karataka, keeping the attacking fist straight, fist inwards and punching with the bottom three knuckles as opposed to the top two. The fist does not turn on impact. The hip twist is a little more pronounced than that of the Karataka.

THE BOXER;

Realising the worth of an efficient jab the Boxer utilises it in 90% of his practice, throwing the punch similarly to his 'Martial' brothers, diverting slightly when he throws the punch from a tight guard and retracts it to a tight guard where it diligently protects the jaw. No 'hikatae' is employed.

The Western Boxing method is the most proficient of the three.

The jabs main use or purpose is to find or manufacture openings in the opponent's defences that the cross or hook punch may engineer, whilst efficiently doing so it also stuns and weakens the opponent. Fast, sharp jabs perform this task, ideally. The harder more powerful jab may be used to hurt or even knock out the opponent, or paradoxically, keep the forward moving opponent at bay.

A practised puncher will easily double or triple the jab, catching the opponent who only anticipates a single punch.

Once the jab has created an opening in the opponent's guard the 'big guns' (cross/hook) may finish the 'job' by manipulating the 'crack' in the opponent's armour.

The text book jab, a mid range punch, is thrown along a straight line from the guard to the target employing a small hip twist on impact. It is a 'stinging' punch with limited scope and range.

LONG RANGE JAB;

To augment the range and scope of the jab, amassing more power, speed and distancing, throw the same punch along the same line adding maximum hip twist on impact with the target (illus). As full hip twist is attained push the stomach (hara) forward, at a 45 degree angle, to enhance the over all effectiveness of the punch.

SHORT RANGE JAB; The short range jab is executed with the same body motion as the long range jab, though with less arm extension The onus being placed almost entirely upon body weight transference. Because lack of distancing disqualifies major arm movement the feeling is one of throwing the whole body at the target as opposed to the body and the arm, there is almost no arm movement (see illus).

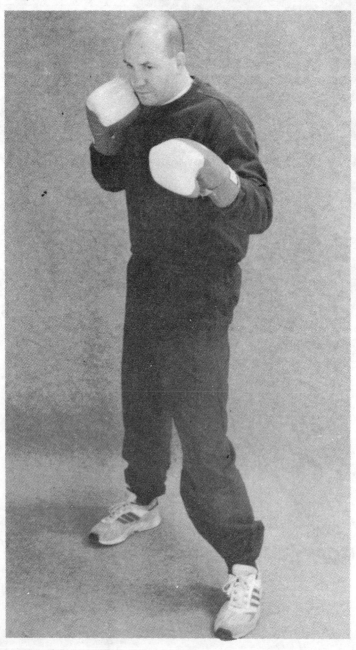

RIGHT LEAN JAB; If you lean your body forward, down and to your own right the jab may be thrown in an upward motion, through the opponent's guard to the 'under' chin'. This catches many opponents by surprise, they only expect the jab to be thrown from the traditional 'on guard' position. (see illus)

LEFT LEAN JAB; By leaning the body forward, down and to your own left the jab may, again, be thrown from an unexpected angle at the opponent's under chin. due to the extreme angle the jabber must execute the punch by straightening the back right leg and (to a lesser degree) the left leg. It is not advised to twist the fist on impact with the target (the under chin or the body) because of the acute angle of the body.

In practice the jab should be worked 4-5 times more than the other punches. When shadow boxing (practising punches in to the air) practice may be abetted by holding a small (3-5 lb) punching weight in the jabbing hand.

CHAPTER FOUR

RIGHT CROSS

The right cross, it would appear, is the fighting worlds most favoured punch, the 'knock out' punch that commands power when ever it is thrown. Much over used by the Martial Arts contest fighter (reverse punch, gyakasuki) due to its notoriously 'safe' point scoring qualities. Paradoxically, even the street fight scenario seems dominated by its bastardised 'brothers'.

For the right handed fighter it is, naturally, the punch to apply, the 'old faithful' syndrome prevails when the 'heat is on'.

In the self defence situation the right cross has been my faithful and reliable compatriot for the last ten years, the punch that I always called upon when the going got a little tough, toted like a six gun in a Hollywood western.

Through out the different styles the right cross is uncannily similar, minor differences set them apart.

KARATE;
Thrown so often by the Karataka that the application of the reverse punch has become a perfunctory act. Executed from a low/no guard position or, more often, from the hikatae position with the supporting hand retracting sharply to the opposite hip. The retracting fist and the attacking fist turning on impact with the target. The right hip is thrust forward along the same line as the punch to enhance power whilst the right foot is kept firmly flat, to maintain balance. Whilst it does so it also inhibits full hip commitment and stifles fast 'travelling', (moving while attacking).

KUNG-FU;
Very similar technique used here to the Karataka. Kung-fu practitioners are less inclined to employ hikatae and more inclined to allow the right foot (whilst in an orthodox stance) to pivot on its ball promoting greater hip involvement and fast travelling.

He also punches with the bottom three knuckles as opposed to the top two. The fist does not twist on impact with the target.

THE BOXER;

The right cross is savoured by the boxer who will only employ it when a 'good' opportunity arises usually reserved for the knock out or its potential.

The boxers fist position varies according to the distance at which the punch is being thrown.

A short right cross is applied with the straight fist (striking with the two major knuckles) the mid ranged punch sees the fist make a half turn whilst the long range punch exploits a full twist on impact with the target. The twist is used, primarily, to break the opponent's skin.

To be ultimately effective the cross must be explosive, It is at its best when coupled or combined with the jab, or other punches off which it may 'bounce'.

The Martial Artist has a tendency to throw the cross (and the lead hand punch) with the shoulder muscles pulled down (see illus), whilst this keeps the punches smartly uniformed it leaves the chin and head dangerously exposed. Paradoxically the boxer hunches the shoulder and back muscles, whilst this may not do anything for the look of the punch it does offer better protection for and off, the chin. Due to the shoulder hunch the boxer tends to punch from the shoulder rather than the stomach (hara), whilst the boxer may still surmount power within his technique he does not utilise it fully. A compromise, therefore should be quested, one that offers protection with out being power derivative, (see illus).

The chin must be protected during execution of the punch, at the same time the punch should derive from the hara rather than the shoulders. It is advised therefore that the shoulder should be kept hunched for protection but not allowed to dominate so much that the punch is influenced by it, one should consciously punch from the hara until it becomes a reflex action to do so.

As a final thought on the foregoing, a lot of fighters have no conception of the dangers involved in not exercising chin protection, for the non conformist I would advise that they test their wares (more specifically fighting without a good guard) in the ring against a pugilist of repute, I guarantee immediate enlightenment.

RIGHT CROSS;
A most powerful technique (if correctly executed) utilising the entire body weight. Thrown from the back, right leg whilst in orthodox stance. Throw the right fist toward the target (jaw) simultaneously thrusting your right hip forward, along the same route as the punch. Your hip should fully extend and thrust in conjunction with the punches connection of the jaw.

Independent right crosses should be practised and employed, most practitioners of different ryu (style) rely up on the jab to build momentum for the cross, telegraphing it to the opponent, who knows that the cross will be preceded by the jab. Randomly mobilise the cross as an independent punch. This will often penetrate the opponent's guard unopposed due to its unexpectedness.

Against the attacking, forward moving opponent the independent 'cross' is a choice punch, firstly because of the aforementioned unexpectability, secondly because the power of the punch is doubled by the opponent's forward momentum.

Another reason for the utilisation of the independent right (or any independent punch) is that in the 'live' scenario it is most often the first independent punch that dictates the rest of the fight, a 'good one' will end the fight immediately in your favour, a bad first punch may mean defeat or an elongated victory.

It can be very difficult to surmount power in a punch without the momentum assistance of a support punch, much practice at 'throwing it alone' is necessary if independent power and speed is to be attained.

Throwing the punch from a no guard position will be foreign to many. From this position the punch is farther away from the target (jaw) than a punch thrown from a high guard. Whilst the high guard is essential in the controlled environment (dojo, gym) no guard (in the earliest stages of an altercation) is just as important in the uncontrolled arena (the street). Once you raise your guard 'outside' your opponent will immediately be warned of your intentions losing you any opportunity of a surprise, pre-emptive strike, also lessening your probabilities of a knock out, the opponent who is aware of an oncoming punch will prepare (consciously or subconsciously) for its absorption, lessening the impetus of the said punch.

It is fair to say that if you want to be an effective 'no guard' puncher you have to practice the same.

CHAPTER FIVE

HOOKING PUNCHES

The hooking punch is probably the most natural of all punching techniques. Most uncontrolled situations are dominated by wild swinging 'hooks' (most of which miss the target). When control goes out of the window, hooks (great big wild ones) come through the door in abundance.

Paradoxically, despite the natural tendencies of the punch it is, for reasons unknown, a difficult punch to teach in the controlled arena, many failing to grasp the 'mechanics' of the punch.

Once it is mastered it becomes awe inspiringly effective offering much power and speed in close range sparring or fighting. Its knock out potential is far greater than any other punch on the curriculum due to the greater target mass available to it.

K.O.'s are secured when the jaw is struck sharply along/on the jaw line, any where from the ear to the point of the chin, giving an over all target area of about 5-6 inches.

Due to the nature of the straight punch it only has open to it the point of the jaw (unless the opponent is facing away from you) at which to aim, approximately one inch, demanding of the punch, pin point accuracy to secure unconsciousness in the opponent. Because the hooking punch attacks the side of the jaw as opposed to the point it has the full length of the jaw to target, pin point accuracy is therefore not so paramount.

KARATE; The Karataka very rarely throws a hook punch, though they can be found in their multitude within Kata (some times 'hidden' within) they are not taught openly on the curriculum.

The hooks within the Kata are utilised in much the same way as all Karate punches, shoulders down, support arm in hikatae. If it were utilised more readily by the Karataka it would become a major part of his armoury. (see illus).

KUNG FU; Much the same here as the Karataka, though the kung fu player does seem to encourage a greater repertoire of punches that fit nicely in with their practice of continuous sparring, unlike the Karataka who opts for the 'stop, start' method.

THE BOXER; It is well known that the boxer greatly favours the hooking punch, (even famed for it). Thrown from the high guard position and retracted to the same. The amateur boxer throws the hook utilising good body weight transference with the punching elbow on the same level as the fist (see illus) twisting the fist on impact with the target so that the palm of the punching hand is facing downwards. The professional boxer throws the hook with the punching elbow slightly lower than the fist (see illus), the fist does not twist on impact, the palm faces in to the puncher's own body. Both methods are equally effective, it is just a case of which one suits.

LEFT HOOK; Thrown from the leading leg of an orthodox stance, a very advanced punch holding great rewards for those who acquire perfection. Aimed ultimately at the opponent's jaw. Very powerful when abetted by the transferred body weight.

All hooking punches are thrown with a direct facsimile to a 'slap', attacking with the knuckles as opposed to the flat of the hand.

For maximum power push your right hip forward and slightly to the left before you strike, keeping your eye on the opponent's jaw.

As you throw the left fist toward the target, pull the hip back to its original position and push your left hip sharply across to your right, following the path of the punch, as it connects with the jaw follow through for maximum effect.

The hip movement will ensure ultimate body weight transference.

RIGHT HOOK; A very powerful, accessible punch, applied again with the facsimile of a 'slap' using the knuckles as opposed to the flat of the hand, to attack. Thrown from the back right leg (whilst in orthodox stance).

Throw the punch from the outside in a semi circular motion towards the target, simultaneously thrust the right hip sharply forward, following the route of the punch.

As it connects with the jaw follow through with the hip and fist for maximum effect.

As with all punches hooks should be practised from the 'on guard' and the 'no guard' position. In the street hooks may be used as a first line attack because of the aforementioned K.O. qualities, in the dojo or gym however they are more effective when assisted by straight punches, more specifically the jab. which will find or make routes of entry in the opponent's armoury.

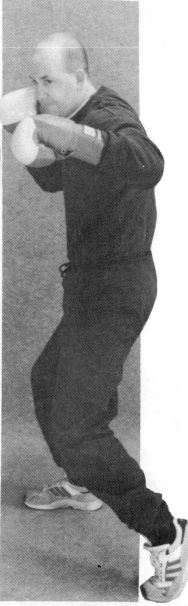

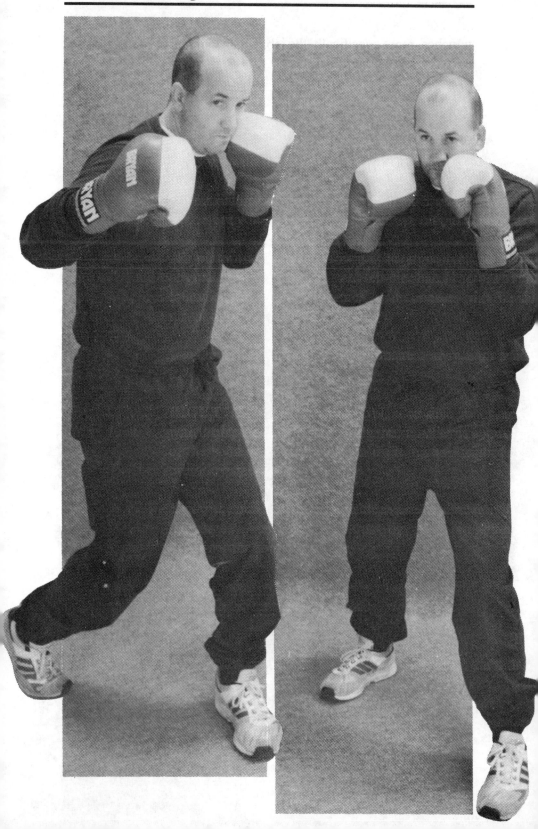

CHAPTER SIX

UPPERCUTS

A wonderful punch with great power and accessibility to the advanced puncher. This is not a punch for the novice.

To be effective the uppercut requires excellent timing and good body control, due to the close proximity that is needed for the employment of this punch it also takes a lot of courage to attempt it, it is likely that the neophyte puncher may get 'hit' en route.

KARATE;

The uppercut emerges through out Kata, though the punch is not on the teaching curriculum, it is almost unheard of for the traditional karataka to employ the uppercut, to do so in competition would likely end in disqualification.

KUNG FU;

Utilised more readily by the kung fu player than the Karataka, though again, not nearly enough.

THE BOXER;

The uppercut is the fourth of the punches employed by the boxer. Because of the high skill factor only the more advanced player utilises it to its full potential.

The versatility of the uppercut allows it to sneak through minute gaps in the opponent's armoury where other punches would find no room. It may be utilised at short range or long range, to the body or the head. The advanced player scores many K.O.'s with this punch, due to the large target area open to it and because it is thrown in an upwards motion out side of the opponent's eye line, it often strikes the target undetected and unopposed.

It may be directed through the centre of the opponent's guard or, as a simultaneous counter attack, inside or underneath the opponent's attacking arm (see illus).

LEFT UPPERCUT;
Thrown from the leading left leg of an orthodox stance aimed, ultimately, at the opponent's jaw. Very powerful if correctly engaged.

For maximum power push your right hip forward and to your left before you strike, slightly bending at the knees so that you are just below the level of the target (jaw). Throw your left fist forward, twisting the punch on impact with the jaw so that the palm of the punching hand is facing inwards (to your own body), simultaneously retract your right hip sharply to its original position and push upwards from your crouched position, thrust your left hip forward and upward, following the route of the punch. On connection with the jaw, follow through with the punch and the hip for maximum effect. (see illus)

RIGHT UPPERCUT;

Thrown from the back right leg, whilst in orthodox stance. Bend slightly at the knees so that you are just below the level of the target (jaw). Throw your right fist upward, twisting the fist on impact with the jaw, so that the palm is facing inwards (to your own body), simultaneously push upward from your crouched position and sharply thrust your right hip forward and upward following the same route as the punch. On connection with the target follow through with the punch and the hip for maximum effect. For the street scenario the uppercut should be practised from a no guard position. It may also be successfully implemented with the aid of the supporting hand, used to pull the opponent, via his attire, into the blow. (see illus).

BREATHING;

With all the aforementioned punching techniques correct 'breathing' is essential. One should exhale through the nose or mouth (either will suffice) as you throw the chosen punch. This will regulate the breathing, feed the working muscles with oxygen and greatly enhances 'Kime'.

CHAPTER SEVEN

FOOTWORK

Footwork, to the puncher, is as consequential as the punching its self, paradoxically, bad footwork will stem the flow of his work like a clot in an artery.

In principle the basic steps are easy, working the steps in conjunction with your hands is another matter, entirely. A great deal of practice is necessary if competence is to be sought. Footwork should be smooth and the steps small if the feet are to compliment the hands. The shoulder width gap, between left foot and right, should, at all times be retained, at no time should the feet meet. If you are attacked whilst the feet are together you will be easily knocked off balance, or over, it is also unpractical to launch an attack from such an unstable position. For light, swift and smooth movement keep on the balls of your feet whilst moving.

FOOTWORK, ORTHODOX STANCE;
When moving around to the left, or simply to the left, move the left foot to your left followed smartly by the right (see illus).

When moving around to the right, or simply to the right, move the right foot to your right followed smartly by the left (see illus).

When moving forwards, move the left foot forward followed smartly by the right (see illus).

When moving backwards move the right foot back followed smartly by the left (see illus). If you move in any other way than above it is likely that the feet will meet and stability will be lost.

Whichever direction you wish to move, the same side of your body should lead, left foot to left side, right foot to right side etc. The feet should gently glide along the surface of the floor as opposed to actually leaving the floor.

It is not advised to punch or attack at the same time as you are moving laterally. If you are moving forward, towards the opponent, attacking is safe (travelling), if you are moving backwards, attacking whilst you move is difficult though still safe (Defensive fighting).

It is also possible to attack whilst moving around, laterally, to the left using the jab with out impairing balance, though the skill factor is high. Using crosses or hooks, however, whilst moving laterally WILL impair balance and is not to be recommended, better to stop and find stability before attempting such attacks.

Moving around, or straight to the right offers no 'safe' opportunities to strike whilst on the move, right lateral movement, therefore, should be reserved for fast evasion or repositioning. The general rule with footwork is 'move, stop, strike'.

Correct footwork should be practised, at first, slowly and meticulously until perfection is attained. Practice moving around a punch bag, or a stationary partner, without throwing a punch. First, clockwise, then anti clock wise, towards the bag then away from it, always being sure to move the correct foot first, according to which direction you wish to move in, if you move the wrong foot the 45 degree stance, and thus balance, will be lost, the feet may meet or cross, impeding you even more. Regular practice should see the transition from position to position performed in a smooth, sharp, efficient manner.

Once you feel capable with the fundamentals of footwork tie it in with single punches, double punches and eventually, combinations, soon the hands and feet will be as one.

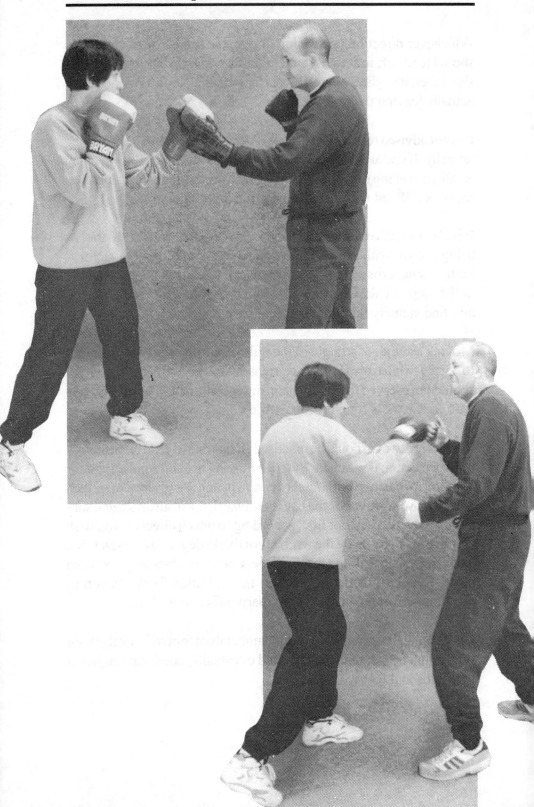

CHAPTER EIGHT

ANGULAR PUNCHES

Having trained in fighting arts all of my life I have always had a reasonable knowledge of 'punching' so I was intrigued whenever I watched the boxing on the T.V. to see punches being thrown that were completely foreign to me. I knew what a 'hook' and a uppercut was, I recognised the jab and cross, but what were those punches that fell in between? Not quite a cross though neither a hook. not quite a hook though neither an uppercut. The people who I asked, some, proficient boxers, didn't know, either, though they threw the same punches instinctively. Through my own research I discovered that they (the unknown punches) were angular or cross punches, bastardisations of the straight, hook or uppercut, two punches mingled in to one. A slight hook on a straight right cross would find an opening in the opponent's defence that the straight cross or full hook would not.

Angling punches, I soon found, meant that any opening, crack or crevice in the opponent's armoury could be manipulated by tailoring a punch to fit the said gap.

Basic punching, (non diversification of the original three, straight, hooked, uppercut), is, metaphorically, a little like a shoe shop that only caters for three sizes of shoe, this is all well and good if you belong to one of these shoe sizes, if not the shop loses its usability, and so it is with punching, whilst there are openings for the three major punches all is fine, if there are no openings your hands become redundant as attacking tools. If, however, you learn the mechanics of angular punches, instead of three lines of attack you end up with an infinite amount, then, no gap in the opponent's defence, no matter how acute the angle, is beyond reaching.

If you look at the graph of angular punches you will see exactly what I mean, and the direct relationship between the punches. Also the points on the graph where one punch comes closer to being another or actually transforms into another, a cross in to a hook, a hook in to an uppercut. etc. Confused? *Let me enlarge on the graph . . .*

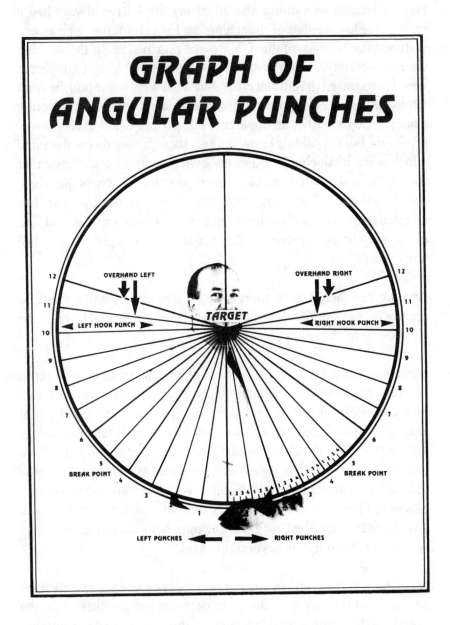

'0' on the graph represents the straight punch, left or right, and the conventional uppercut, left or right.

'10' represents the conventional hook punch, left or right.

'11' and '12' represent the overhand right or left hook.

All the numbers in between, from '1'-'9' represent angled variations of the three conventional punches.

The left side of the graph represents left punch variations, the right side of the graph, right punch variations.

In the case, as a for instance, of the conventional right cross, it starts out as a straight punch which travels along the line between '0' and 'target'. If that route to target is obstructed by a tight guard the puncher may chose to throw the cross along angle No '1', adding a slight hook to the cross, if No '1' does not offer a great enough angle to take the punch around the opponent's guard he may chose to throw the punch along angle '2', '3' or '4'. All of these punches would be classed as 'hooked crosses', the hook becoming more prominent the higher the number angle that you chose.

No '5' on the graph is the 'break point', this is where the cross becomes more hooked than straight and is therefore classed as a 'crossed hook', as the angle becomes more great, 6, 7, 8 etc. the punch becomes more and more hooked until, at angle '10' it transforms in to a conventional right hook. This may be reversed, the chosen punch may start as a conventional right hook, travelling along the line from angle 10 to target. As the punch comes down the scale and the angle decreases it reaches break point at angle 5 and then becomes more and more straight, until at angle 0 it, again becomes the conventional straight right cross.

The system works the same with the conventional right uppercut, which starts, traditionally, at angle '0', as the angle increases up the number scale so does the degree of hook in the punch, up to angle 4 all of these punches would be classed as 'hooked uppercuts'. At angle 5 break point, the punch becomes more hook than uppercut and so, between 5 & 9 the punches are classed as 'uppercut hooks'. At angle 10 we are back to the conventional right hook. Angle 11 & 12 are overhand right hooks (or left hooks on the left side of the scale). An overhand hook is a punch that is thrown above the opponent's head and guard then 'dropped' downwards on to the target.

The left side of the scale deals with the left jab, hook and uppercut, all are thrown from the left lead leg (whilst in orthodox stance).

The left hook and uppercut are performed with an exact facsimile to the right hook and uppercut, on the right side of the scale. The left jab works the same as the right cross, starting conventionally, along angle '0' to target. From angle 1- 4 the punch would be classed as a 'hooked jab', angle '5', break point, to angle '9' the punch becomes more hooked than straight and is therefore classed as a 'jabbed hook'.

As a final point on 'angles' you will notice on the graph, between numbers 1-5, in between each major angle number, minor angle numbers, along which less deviated punches may be thrown.

Almost every punch that you throw will vary slightly in angle from the last, deeming every punch different. This gives you a limitless choice of punches from which to chose, all born from the conventional, hook, straight and uppercut.

Add to the angle graph the 'distancing graph' and, again all of the punches take on a new context.

The most common punching range is No 3, mid range. Most fighters feel competent and safe at this distance. Long and short range punches are also utilised (though less so) at some time, by most fighters. All distances are beneficial to the puncher. It is fair to say that the more powerful blows are thrown at mid range.

The long and short range punches demand a higher skill factor to transfer body weight behind the blow.

The smaller lines, in between the major angles (1-5) represent minor ranges in between the three principle.

STRAIGHT PUNCHES. JAB & CROSS;

The short to long range jab is executed as formerly described in chapter 3, the jab. The right cross varies very little between short and long range, the hip twist behind the punch and the swivel on the ball of the right foot to aid the twist is the same throughout the ranges, though mid to long range does benefit more from the body weight transference and momentum than the shorter ranges. On the short range cross, the fist does not twist on impact with the target, the major two knuckles are used to strike but the palm of the attacking hand remains inwards. The longer the range of the punch the more the fist turns until, at full range the fist turns completely with the palm of the attacking hand facing downward.

HOOK PUNCHES;

The short range hook requires very little arm movement and major body movement if power is to be attained.

The right arm (right hook) is thrown directly from the guard to the target lifting the right elbow to assist, the fist turns just enough to ensure that the two major knuckles strike the target. The further the hook travels along the distancing graph the more the punching arm straightens and the attacking fist turns, until, at long range, No 5, the arm is straight and the wrist of the punching fist is bent so acutely that the palm is facing towards your own body. Alternatively, on the long range hook, you may keep the wrist straight, turning the palm outwards, (see illus) away from the target, striking again with the two major knuckles.

UPPERCUT;

The uppercut may be thrown in two ways, upward, as its title implies, or straight.

The straight uppercut is thrown in the same genre as the straight cross, with the palm of the fist facing upwards as opposed to inwards or downwards.

The basic technique of the traditional uppercut is as describe in Chapter Six, Uppercuts.

It may be thrown at short range, from a very tight guard, which restricts body weight transference The palm of the attacking hand turns inwards (to your own body) on impact with the target. As the punch reaches the longer distances it becomes necessary for the wrist of the attacking fist to bend more and more inwards to enable the puncher to strike with the two major knuckles. At No 5, long range on the distancing graph, the wrist bend will be extremely acute.

The advanced player will combine all of the aforementioned, instinctively.

To practice angular punches (at various ranges) use a punch bag and go 'around the clock' with your chosen punch. Starting perhaps with a straight right cross, With each consecutive punch add a slight angle (or hook) until you reach break point (No 5 on the angular graph) where the punch becomes more of a hook than a cross, continue adding angle until you reach the conventional 'hook' (No 10 on the angular graph), adding more angle after the conventional hook will give you the 'overhand right' (No 11 & 12 on the angular graph). Practice 'around the clock' with all of your punches, vary the ranges, short, medium, long etc.

You can also practice 'angular' in the air (shadow boxing) in the same 'around the clock' manner.

CHAPTER NINE

DRAWING TECHNIQUES

*"COME IN TO MY PARLOUR,
SAID THE SPIDER TO THE FLY."*

Drawing (not with a pencil) is the art of tempting or coercing an opponent in to a trap by means of tactical play. A little like chess where you lead your opponent to believe that you have made a mistake by deliberately sacrificing a pawn, he takes advantage of the 'supposed' error by 'taking' your offering not realising that by doing so he has left his king unprotected.

This may be achieved by two methods. The first method is to show the opponent a gap in your defence by dropping or lifting your guard exposing the target that you wish to 'offer' as bait in the hope that the opponent will take the sacrifice and attack the exposed area. When (if) he does, you penalise him by attacking him as he is about to take the bait.

For instance, If I raise my guard slightly, exposing my abdomen as 'bait' my opponent, believing this to be a tactical error on my part, attempts to attack the opening with a low right cross (as illus) as he moves in to do so I attack his jaw with a right cross of my own. The opponent is so keen to take advantage of my 'error' that he fails to see my trap. You may even let the opponent 'take' the bait once or twice to lull him in to a false sense of security, then, when he least expects it, release the trap.

Another coercement is to feign tiredness or injury tempting your opponent to 'come in for the kill', as he does so suddenly launch an unexpected attack catching him unawares.

Throwing weak techniques (some of us do not have to feign this) at an opponent also encourages him to come forward with counter attacks, happy in the belief that he will not get hurt because your technique is 'weak'. For instance, throwing a sloppy, weak jab will encourage your opponent to throw, perhaps, a right cross counter punch, because you are expecting the counter it will be easy to 'slip' countering or pre-empting it with a left hook to his now exposed chin. If you throw a half hearted right cross it will encourage the opponent to move forward to counter, as he does so pre-empt him with a left hook.

There are various techniques which will 'draw' an opponent, many of them depend upon the genre of fighter in front of you. If he is a forward moving offensive fighter weak, drawing punches would effectively lure him in to 'bigger' techniques. If he is a backward moving defensive fighter offer him an 'opening' in your defence or feign tiredness/injury to encourage him to be offensive.

The best way to perfect these techniques is in actual sparring where experimenting with different methods will show you what does and does not work. Every fighter is different, what may work on one may fail abysmally on another, the only way to find out and perfect is to try.

CHAPTER TEN

FEINTS

Bruce Lee once said that when two fighters of equal ability meet, the master of the feint will victor.

The feint is brothers with drawing techniques, both are tactical ploys to manufacture 'openings' in an opponent's defence. The latter does so by encouraging the opponent to attack an opening that isn't really there, manipulating the opening left by the opponent's irrationality. The former, creates openings in the opponent's defence by pretending to attack one area of the opponent's body, thus drawing his guard to the said attack and then throwing a real attack to the gap left by the falsely deployed guard.

This may be achieved by feigning a low blow to draw the opponent's guard down, long enough for you to manipulate the 'high' opening left, or by feigning a high blow, drawing the opponent's guard upwards, long enough for you to strike the manufactured 'low' opening.

The feint blow and the intended blow may be any of your choosing, as long as they flow, and the intended blow fits in to the opening created by your feint, for instance, it would be futile to create a high opening with a low feint only to employ another low punch as your intended one.

You may use any combination that fits the circumstances, experimenting with different methods will unearth many variations.

Because the feint draws the guard away from the area that it is meant to protect, the intended blow, especially the high face punch, has the potential to finish the fight, not so much because the target area has been left unprotected, more because the falsely deployed guard (and the opponent's mind) believes that the feint punch is a real one and thus is too pre occupied with it to see the intended blow, which goes through completely unchallenged by the unprepared recipient. As formerly stated, it is the unseen blow that causes most damage because the body cannot prepare for the blow that it does not see.

It is good practice, when using a feint, to first actually strike and hurt the opponent by fully committing the blow once or twice before you employ it as a feint, the opponent is far more likely to deploy his guard to block a punch that has already hit and hurt him, and, because up until that point you have not used the punch as a feint he will lulled all the more in to a false sense of security.

The feints greatest attribute is the fact that, because people block as an instinctive reaction, the same feint may be used again and again on the same opponent who will automatically try to block it, even, if and when they don't want to.

Here are a few to savour.

In all of the forthcoming techniques the first named is the feint punch and the second named is the intended punch.

LOW LEFT JAB, HIGH RIGHT CROSS;
This combination is ideal for a knock out because, if successful the jab feint exposes the opponent's jaw to the 'big' right cross.

Firstly, throw a couple of hard left jabs to the opponent's body, when he responds by lowering his guard to block, throw a fast half jab just close enough to the target to entice the opponent's guard down, almost simultaneously throw the right cross to the opponent's exposed jaw. The most important factor here is to follow the feint almost simultaneously with the right cross, any delay and the intended punch will be easily spotted and thus blocked. An experienced player will deploy the opponent's guard with a simple flick of the shoulder (left or right, depending upon the feint you wish to actuate) which, to the defender, will appear to be the beginnings of an actual attack.

HIGH LEFT JAB, LOW RIGHT CROSS/HOOK;
This is an exact antipodal of the previous combination. Throwing a high left jab to draw the opponent's guard upward thus exposing his

rib and abdomen area to your right cross. Firstly, throw and score with a few stiff left jabs, when the opponent reacts by raising his guard to block your jab throw a sharp half jab towards his face, just close enough to convince the opponent that it is a real blow, (it isn't necessary to score with the feint punch, only to convince the opponent that you are trying to) then, almost simultaneously, throw a strong right cross to the opponent's exposed abdomen/rib area.

DOUBLE JAB;

No matter how many times you use this combination it works, even on the same opponent. If and when he finally does become accustomed to the double jab and its effectiveness wanes you may add another jab parenting the 'triple jab', and it will 'work' again. As with the other combinations, initially build the opponent's reaction with hard, hurting single jabs, when you are happy that the opponent's reaction is sufficient, throw a sharp, half jab just close enough to the target to gain the desired reaction, then almost simultaneously double up with the intended jab (see illus).

LOW RIGHT CROSS, HIGH LEFT HOOK;

Aim the low right cross at the opponent's rib/abdomen area, a couple of hard hitting shots will catalyse a marked reaction from the opponent whose guard will 'drop' in an attempt to engage the cross. When the reaction is sufficient throw a sharp half cross to the body, close enough to manufacture the desired reaction, the almost simultaneously, throw a high left hook to the opponent's exposed jaw.

LOW LEFT JAB, HIGH LEFT HOOK;

A difficult combination with a high skill factor, paradoxically, if perfected it has excellent K.O potential.

Throw a couple of hard hitting jabs to the opponent's rib/abdomen area to cause a reaction in his guard, when the reaction is sufficient and his guard is moving down to engage the punch throw a sharp half jab towards the opponent's mid section the, almost simultaneously retract the left hand and attack over the opponent's descending guard with the intended left hook striking his exposed jaw.

Care must be taken with this combination to avoid the opponent's right cross, if he releases it as you are moving in to employ your left hook, you will meet it head on.

There are of course many more feints than the few aforementioned. Experiment and find the ones that work for you.

CHAPTER ELEVEN

COMBINATIONS

Combination punching is not as easy as you would imagine, it is an acquired art. Each punch of any given combination must flow smoothly with the last and the next, whilst still retaining balance, utilising body weight transference, timing, distancing, accuracy etc. etc. Each punch should, automatically seek out an open and vulnerable target. Combinations (and similar punches) are wasted if they strike the opponent's guard or non vulnerable areas like the highly muscular back or chest.

In order that the combinations flow they must go with as opposed to the body's mechanics, each punch should prime the next. For instance, a right hook would not flow if it followed a right cross, a left hook would.

Ultimately one should aim to achieve 'automatic' combinations, where the body feels out parties of punches without the restriction of conscious thought, for the brain to do this it must have multifarious combinations programmed into it, a little like data in a computer's memory bank, when you press recall on the keyboard the computer feeds out the stored data, automatically. Feed the various combinations into your own memory banks, then, when the situation 'demands' it will also 'feed out' automatically.

The key to learning combinations is to start small, combinations of two punches will suffice in the beginning, build to three or four, five, six and so on. Also, practice as many different variations of the 2, 3, 4, 5 and 6 punch combinations as you can so that eventually. your memory bank will be holding so many that it will be able to mix and intermingle all the different combinations to suit the various opponents or situations, giving you, ultimately, an infinite number of different variations of the originals.

To start with I shall list several combinations that I personally practice and teach, you must enlarge on these and develop more of your own.

All the forthcoming combinations may be aimed to the body, head, or an association of both. For them to be effective there should be no gap, stutter or stop between each blow, each consecutive punch takes advantage of the opening in the opponent's guard created by the previous punch, if it is in any way delayed (stutters or stops) the said opening will close before it can be utilised, thus neutralising the punch.

1. LEFT JAB, RIGHT CROSS. (2)

2. LEFT JAB, RIGHT HOOK. (2)

3. RIGHT CROSS, LEFT HOOK. (2)

4. LEFT HOOK, RIGHT CROSS. (2)

5. RIGHT CROSS, LEFT UPPERCUT. (2)

6. LEFT UPPERCUT, RIGHT CROSS. (2)

7. RIGHT UPPERCUT, LEFT HOOK. (2)

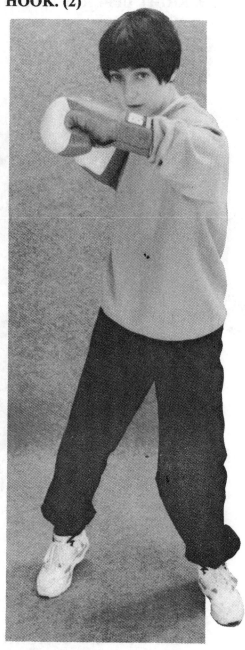

8. LEFT JAB, RIGHT CROSS, LEFT HOOK. (3)

9. RIGHT UPPERCUT, LEFT HOOK, RIGHT HOOK. (3)

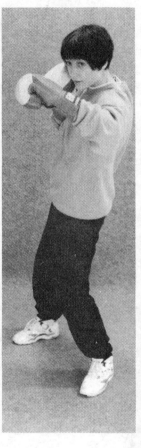

10. LEFT UPPERCUT, RIGHT CROSS, LEFT HOOK. (3)

11. RIGHT CROSS, LEFT HOOK, RIGHT UPPERCUT. (3)

12. LEFT JAB, RIGHT CROSS, LEFT UPPERCUT, RIGHT UPPERCUT. (4)

13. RIGHT CROSS, LEFT UPPERCUT, RIGHT HOOK, LEFT HOOK, RIGHT CROSS. (6)

14. LEFT JAB, RIGHT CROSS, LEFT JAB RIGHT CROSS, LEFT JAB, RIGHT CROSS. (6)

15. LEFT UPPERCUT, RIGHT UPPERCUT, LEFT HOOK, RIGHT HOOK, LEFT JAB, RIGHT CROSS, LEFT HOOK. (7)

As you can see, the combination possibilities are infinite. Note also how each consecutive punch flows with the last and leaves the body ideally positioned for the next punch. For instance, in combination No 10. the first punch leaves the puncher's hip to the extreme right, ideally situated for the right cross. The right cross leaves the hip fully extended forward, ideally positioned for the left hook. Try to construct your own combinations, similarly.

Bag work is the best method of practising combination punching. Start off lightly with small combinations, gradually, over a period of time (several months) build the combinations. Ultimately, try ad-libbing combinations, see how many punches that you can throw without stopping or breaking the flow.

At first this will prove to be very difficult, in time, however, it will become easier, eventually an automatic response.

CHAPTER TWELVE

DEFENCES AND COUNTER ATTACKS

Knowing how to attack is all fine and well, but, it is only 50% of the needed curriculum. The other 50% is defence work, knowing how to avoid being hit your self and counter attacking the blows you have managed to evade/block. Once these blocks and evasions have been learned to a reasonable standard you, the defender, may incorporate attacks/counter attacks in to the blocks and evasions so as to take full advantage of the attacker who, momentarily leaves him self open for attack/counter attack whilst he is busy attacking, himself.

Never lose sight of the fact that whilst defence is very important, it is attack that is the best means of defence (especially in the self defence scenario).

DEFENCE AND COUNTER ATTACKS AGAINST THE JAB;
There are several defences against the jab.

1. LEAD HAND PARRY;
As the jab comes towards your face parry it across to your right with the palm of the left lead hand. It is important with this parry, and all parries, not commit the parrying hand too much in case the attack is thrown by the opponent as a ploy/feint to falsely deploy your guard.

COUNTER ATTACKS;
Counter with a right cross, hook or if you are sharp, a counter jab with the left, parrying hand. Target the body or the head. (see illus)

2. REVERSE HAND PARRY; As the jab comes towards your face parry it across to your left with the palm of your right hand.

COUNTER ATTACKS; Counter with a left jab, hook or uppercut, according to the opening in the opponent's defence. (see illus)

3. GUARD BLOCK; As the jab comes towards your face or body, close your guard by touching left hand and right hand, elbow to elbow in front of your own face and body taking the force of the blow on your arms.

COUNTER ATTACKS; Counter with any punch, but preferably the left jab or right cross for safety, speed and accessibility. (see illus).

4. LEFT SHOULDER BLOCK;

As the jab comes towards your face lift your left shoulder, high, simultaneously rolling the left side of your upper body inwards, parrying the left jab with the shoulder. (as illus)

5. THE DUCK; Bend at the knees so that you drop underneath the attacking jab, be sure not to bend at the torso, this could prove dangerous to you due to loss of visibility.

COUNTER ATTACKS; It is only effectively possible to counter with low body shots, the left jab, right cross and left hook being most accessible.

6. THE SLIP; The slip may be employed to the left or to the right. As the jab comes towards your face slip it by moving your head inside the jab, to your right, or outside the jab, to your left.

COUNTER ATTACKS; Right slip; Counter with a left jab, uppercut or hook (body or head) or a right hook (body or head). Left slip; Counter with a right cross or hook (body or head) or a left jab, hook or uppercut (body or head). Counter attacks that compliment the slip may and should be executed simultaneously with the slip, hitting the opponent as he is moving in with his attack. (see illus).

7. LAY BACK; As the jab comes towards your face move backwards and out of the punches range by transferring your weight from the lead left leg (whilst in orthodox stance) to the back right leg, bending it enough to take you out of range.

COUNTER ATTACKS; Counter with a left jab, hook or uppercut, either simultaneously with the 'lay back' (see illus) or as the opponent is retracting the jab. You may also counter attack with a right cross or hook, wait until the opponent is retracting the jab before you launch your counter, transfer the weight back on to the front leg so that you are back in orthodox stance and counter with the chosen blow.

8. STEP BACK;
As the jab comes towards your face step slightly backwards with the right rear leg, just enough to take you out of the jab's range.

COUNTER ATTACKS;
As with the lay back, the step back counters may be employed simultaneously with the step back, catching the attacker as he moves in, or after, when the opponent is extracting the jab. Be sure to move back to orthodox stance as you throw your chosen counter. Left jab/hook/uppercut and right cross/hook are all worthy contenders for counter attack after the step back evasion.

The defences employed for the neutralisation of the jab are, in the main, a facsimile for those used to block/evade the other punches (cross, uppercut, hook). where they are the same please refer to the forgoing for the greater details and mechanics of the moves.

DEFENCE AGAINST THE RIGHT CROSS;
Being a straight punch the right cross defences are a facsimile to the left jab defences, where differences do occur I shall digress.

LEAD HAND PARRY;
As the jab comes towards your face parry it across to your right with the palm of the left lead hand, do not over commit the parry in case the 'cross' is a ploy/feint.

COUNTER ATTACKS;
You may counter attack with a right cross to the opponent's face over the top of the attacker's extended right arm, or with a right cross to the body under the attacker's extended right arm. If you are sharp you may throw a counter jab with the parrying hand.

REVERSE HAND PARRY;
As the cross comes towards your face parry it across to your left with the palm of your right hand, simultaneously move your head and shoulders to your right and away from the force of the blow.

COUNTER ATTACKS;

You may counter with a left jab (body or head) or a left hook/uppercut to the body.

GUARD BLOCK;

As the cross comes towards your face or body close the guard by touching left hand to right hand, elbow to elbow in front of your face and body, taking the force of the blow on your arms.

COUNTER ATTACKS;

You may counter with any punch, but preferably the left jab or right cross, for safety, speed and accessibility.

LEFT SHOULDER BLOCK;

As the cross comes towards your face lift your left shoulder high, simultaneously rolling your upper body inwards, parrying the cross with your left shoulder.

COUNTER ATTACKS;

Counter with a left jab or hook, over the opponent's extended right arm to the head, under his arm when countering to the body. Right uppercut is also accessible.

THE DUCK;

Bend at the knees so that you drop underneath the cross. be sure not to bend at the torso.

COUNTER ATTACKS;

It is only effectively possible to counter, from this position, with low body shots. The left jab, right cross and right hook being most accessible.

THE SLIP;

The 'slip' may be employed to the right or the left of the cross. When employing the slip to your left your movement should be more extreme than when slipping to your right, due to the fact that the cross is coming from the right.

COUNTER ATTACKS;
Right slip; Counter with a left jab/uppercut/hook or a right hook (body or head). Left slip; Counter with a right cross/hook or left jab/hook/uppercut (body or head).

Counter attacks that compliment the slip may and should be executed simultaneously with the slip, catching the opponent as he moves in with his attack.

LAY BACK;
As the cross comes towards your face move backwards, out of the punches range by transferring the weight from the lead left leg to the back right leg, bending it just enough to take you out of the punches range.

COUNTER ATTACKS;
You may counter attack with a left jab/hook, which should be employed simultaneously with your lay back, catching the opponent as he moves in to attack, or with a right cross/hook as the opponent retracts the right cross. Be sure to retain the orthodox stance before you throw the right hand as a counter.

STEP BACK;
As the cross comes towards your face step slightly backwards with your right rear leg, taking you just outside of the punches range.

COUNTER ATTACKS;
As with the lay back the step back counter attacks may be applied as you step back and away from the opponent's cross or as the cross is being retracted.

OPEN HAND THRUST;
As soon as the opponent initiates the right cross punch out with your lead left hand and thrust it in to the bend on the opponent's punching

arm (between the biceps and the fore arm) stopping the cross in its tracks. (see illus)

COUNTER ATTACKS;

Ideally, from this position, counter attack with a right cross or hook to the opponent's head or body.

DEFENCE AND COUNTER ATTACKS AGAINST 'HOOKS'.

The most effective defences against the hooking punch are evasive defences as opposed to blocks.

BOB AND WEAVE;

(left or right) Against a right hook, bob below the punch as it comes towards your head, weave to your left and underneath it (see illus).

COUNTER ATTACKS;
After weaving underneath the punch, counter attack with a left jab or hook to the opponent's body or head. Against the left hook; bob below the punch as it comes towards your head, weave to your right and underneath it.

COUNTER ATTACKS;
After weaving underneath the punch, counter attack with a right cross, hook or uppercut (body or head). If you aim the right uppercut counter to the opponent's head you will need to direct the blow underneath the opponent's extended left arm.

The guard block, duck, lay back, step back and open hand thrust defences, formerly described, (and their counter attacks) may all, also be successfully used in defence of the hooking punch with the exact facsimile as the jab or cross.

DEFENCE AND COUNTER ATTACKS AGAINST THE UPPERCUT;
There are only one or two successful and worth while defences against this devious punch.

1. GUARD BLOCK;
As the punch comes towards your head or body close your guard by touching left hand to right hand, elbow to elbow, in front of your face and body, taking the force of the blow on your arms.

COUNTER ATTACKS;
You may counter with any punch, but preferably the left jab or right cross for safety, speed and accessibility. Due to the close proximity of the attacking uppercut your chosen counter attacks must, out of necessity, be short range punches.

NOTE; *WITH ALL OF THE FOREGOING COUNTER ATTACKS, IF THE OPENING IN THE OPPONENT'S ARMOURY ALLOWS, THROW A COMBINATION OF PUNCHES TO FOLLOW THE*

INITIALLY CHOSEN COUNTER ATTACK, AS OUTLINED IN CHAPT. 11 COMBINATIONS.

The more that you work with the foregoing techniques the more familiar, effective and instinctive they will become. You will discover the defences and counter attacks that suit you best as an individual, tailoring them to your needs. Feel free to experiment and develop your own variations of those previously outlined, as long as they work and do not open up your vulnerability.

Practice the blocks and counter attacks in a controlled environment before testing them (and yourself) out for 'real'. The controlled practice of all techniques is an important part of confidence building.

CHAPTER THIRTEEN

HAND SPARRING

This is where you road test all of the techniques that you have been (or should have been) practising so diligently. BEWARE!! When it comes to free sparring don not rush in. Walk before you try to run. I have witnessed many good potential punchers receive decimated egos because they attempted 'too much too soon'. Pyramid your sparring, start at the bottom with light sparring or even restricted sparring (a detailed explanation of the various sparring methods can be found further into the chapter).

As your confidence and skill increases so should the severity of your sparring, until you progress to 'full contact' sparring wearing 16 oz boxing gloves. If you jump in to the deep end right from the start it is likely that your progress will be slow, believe me, if you think you are going to get trounced every time you make a mistake (which is probable in full contact sparring) you will not take any chances and try out new techniques, relying up on the moves that you know will work for you. So, better to start off light.

When you do become proficient enough to enter the 'full contact' arena do not discard 'light' or 'restricted sparring. As an advanced player there is still much to be gained from their practice and always some thing to learn.

There are 4 different types of hand sparring (or boxing).
1. Pre-set sparring.
2. Restricted sparring.
3. Light skill sparring.
4. Heavy sparring.

Be you a beginner or an advanced player, all four should be practised regularly.

PRE-SET SPARRING;
This is the foundation of advanced technique. All of the punches, defences and counter attacks described in the former chapters may be practised and perfected in pre-set sparring.

Pre-set is practised with a partner who lightly attacks with a pre chosen punch, jab, cross etc. As the defender you evade or block the said punch and counter attack with another. For instance, your opponent and your self face off in the pre described 45 degree stance (orthodox or south paw). The attacker attacks with a left jab, as the jab comes towards your face execute a left, lead hand parry to deflect the jab, counter attack with a right cross counter to the opponent's head (with control).

Reverse the play, you attack with a left jab whilst your opponent defends and counter attacks. This should be practised with multifarious attacks, defences and counter attacks until competence is formed and confidence gained.

Once the former and latter are in residence the ferocity of the pre-set practice should increase until the attacker is aiming a full contact blow, hitting the defender if he fails to block or evade.

The counter attacks, however should always be controlled because they are not defended against.

Any attack, block and counter attack may be employed in pre-set sparring, as long as the chosen techniques are agreed upon before hand.

Again, as confidence and ability grows, the defender may and should try to add lib his defence and counter attacks, this will develop automatic reaction.

Pre-set sparring is a good confidence builder, it also develops competence to excellence in attack, defence and counter attack whilst greatly enhancing distancing. It is a gentle introduction to sparring for the beginner and an excellent way for the advanced player to perfect senior moves.

RESTRICTED SPARRING;

Restricted sparring may be practised light or heavy, fast or slow, it is, as its title suggests, restricted. This may mean restricted to fighting with only one punch, ie. a left jab, or a right cross. For instance, if the fighters are restricted to a left jab, when they spar that is the only attacking tool they may use. You may also restrict the fighting to 'light' where heavy contact is disallowed or paradoxical, 'heavy' where the participants may strike each other as hard as they wish. This genre of restriction extends itself to all of the punches on the curriculum.

Another form of restriction is to limit one partner to a left jab whilst his opponent may only block and counter attack, again this 'restriction' may be lent to any of the attacks and not only the jab.

Restricted sparring is, in effect, isolating a chosen technique for improvement. If your jab is below standard, for instance, restricted 'jab' sparring will quickly bring it up to scratch.

LIGHT SKILL SPARRING;

Any thing goes here as far as techniques are concerned, with only the exception of heavy contact. Any thing and every thing may be practised in the full knowledge that no matter what mistakes you or your opponent might make, you will not be penalised for it with a heavy blow or counter blow.

Light sparring is the most enjoyable of all sparring methods because the sky is the limit and bloody noses are a rarity. if you want to try that 'left jab, left hook' combination that Joe Louis favoured or the triple left hook famed by 'Sugar ray', then by all means do so, if it goes drastically wrong, nothing is lost (except perhaps the illusion that you thought it would be easy).

Light sparring is where great technique is formulated and nurtured, perhaps thrown a thousand times before perfection is gained, and confidence is built enough to transport you in to the 'full contact arena'. It also allows hours of uninjured practice.

HEAVY SPARRING;
''The proof of pudding is in the eating''

Heavy gloves (12-16 oz) should be worn for protection whilst engaging in heavy sparring.

Whilst pre-set, restricted and light sparring are important and necessary they are of little use with out the additive of 'heavy' all out boxing sparring. You can sit in a learner car and fiddle with the controls for as long as you like, you can drive around a deserted air field or industrial estate until you are blue in the face, and it all helps, but, until you've taken the car out into heavy traffic, you haven't driven.

Getting in to the heavy traffic of all out sparring can be very daunting, but it needs to be done. It is here that you try the practised techniques out on an opponent who is doing like wise, where mistakes may and will be heavily penalised.

Born here is the realisation that, what you get away with in light sparring may not be tolerated in heavy, mistakes can and will prove to be painful (to the mistake). Heavy sparring is the 'pressure test' of technique and character.

This is where the jab (left or right) comes in to its own and, certainly in your first few encounters, you dare not risk trying any thing else.

The straight jab and cross are the bread and butter punches of heavy sparring, much confidence must be sought before trying out the closer range hooks and uppercuts.

'Bottle' is also heavily tested in this uncomfortable arena, blows that get through your defences can be brutal, disorientation is probable, unconsciousness possible. If you do 'catch a good one' and your legs want to give way to gravity it is best not to give in and stop (unless it is absolutely necessary). You may do one of 3 things (4 if you wish to consider 'run for your life' as an option) if things get a little too much.

1. COVER UP;

Tuck your chin deeply in to your chest, lift your shoulders high and close your guard around your face and body as tightly as possible. Take the brunt of the attacking blows on your guard until it is possible to move out of the line of fire, or are able to counter attack, or attack back.

2. GRAB AND HOLD;

Move in close to you opponent and grab him, tuck your face in as close to his body as possible, this will make it awkward for him to hit you with any degree of force. Hold on to him until you are capable of attacking/counter attacking, or of moving out of his punching range.

MOVE;

Use sharp footwork (as described in Chapter 7. Footwork) to evade and keep out of the opponent's punching range until orientation returns and you are capable of fighting back.

Remember, if realism is to be sought heavy sparring should be a regular part of your training schedule.

It is advised by the author to wear protective equipment in light and heavy sparring. 16oz gloves, head gear and gum shield, (box, shin guard, wrist guard, body protector, crash helmet, knife/bullet proof vest, suit of armour, steel toe capped shoes etc. etc. etc; only joking).

CHAPTER FOURTEEN

HANDS AGAINST FEET

J. F. Gilby, in his book '*World Wrestling and Western Boxing*' said that a puncher will always beat a kicker. In the main I believe this to be true, though it takes a lot of working at.

A dominant kicker will destroy any player of any genre if the said player allows the kicker 'space'. It's all about distancing. If you allow the kicker kicking distance he is in his element, you must close him down by moving inside his kicking range, close enough for you to employ punching techniques. The danger involved in 'closing' the kicker down is getting caught doing so, that is walking on to a kick. This can be very damaging because the power of the said kick is doubled when you move forward, on to it. Powerful kickers like David Mears, ex world Martial arts champion who spent three years in Thailand on a Thai boxing camp, will destroy you with one kick if you allow him space. It is better, therefore, to allow the kicker to kick, block or evade the kick and then move inside his kicking range as he retracts the kick, most kickers drop their guard when executing a kicking technique leaving their heads vulnerable to counter attacks.

Turning kicks, ie. round house, back round house etc. are a lot easier to break down than straight kicks, which may penetrate even the tightest guard.

I shall list the most popular kicks, demonstrating how best to break them down.

DEFENCES AGAINST THE FRONT KICK; ELBOW BLOCK;

A strong front kicker can be very dangerous if not quickly dissuaded. As soon as you realise that the opponent is keen to employ the front kick employ the elbow block by striking the shin of the opponent's kicking leg with your left lead elbow. As the kick comes towards your body drop the lead elbow, whilst still retaining the guard, on to the opponent's shin (see illus). Due to the pain inflicting qualities of this block, once is usually enough to persuade the opponent not to use the kick again.

COUNTER ATTACKS;
Counter with a right cross, hook or uppercut.

GEDANBARI;
From orthodox stance block the attacking right leg to the inside of the opponent's calf with the outside of your left wrist, by striking in a downward motion. Simultaneously move your right foot around to your right (be sure, on landing to retain your 45 degree front stance). This will block and deflect the kick away from you.

COUNTER ATTACKS;
Counter with a right cross/hook or uppercut (body or head) Gedanbari to the opponent's left front kick is an almost direct facsimile to blocking the right front kick, the deviance being the fact that you block the opponent's attacking leg on the outside of the shin as opposed to the left side, after the leg has been deflected the opponent will land facing away from you as opposed to facing to you.

COUNTER ATTACKS;
Counter attack with a right cross or hook (body or head) be careful not to strike the opponent's skull (because he has his back to you) this will serve no other purpose than to damage your punching hand.

SOTOBARI;
This is the antipodal of gedanbari, blocking with the inside of the wrist as opposed to the outside.

From orthodox stance, block the attacking right leg on the outside of the calf muscle with the inside of the left wrist by striking in a downward motion, simultaneously move your right foot across, behind and to your own left. As the kick is deflected away from you move your left leg forward and to your left to retain the 45 degree front stance.

COUNTER ATTACKS;
Counter attack with a right cross or hook (body or head).

Sotobari to the opponent's left front kick is almost a direct facsimile to blocking the right front kick, the deviance being that the block strikes the inside of the attacking leg as opposed to the outside, after the opponent's leg has been deflected he will land facing towards you as opposed to away.

COUNTER ATTACKS;
Counter attack with a right cross, hook or uppercut (body or head).

CLOSE DOWN;
In theory the 'close down' is simple, as the opponent initiates his front kick by raising the knee of the attacking leg, move forward and attack with any given punch, catching him mid way through his technique. In practice it is not so simple, demanding perception, excellent timing and 'guts'. As formerly mentioned, moving on to a straight kick can prove to be very painful.

An experienced kicker like Ian McCranor commonwealth silver medalist (or Peter Consterdine who kicks Elephants to death with his kicks) who reads your intentions may use the knee lift to 'draw' you in, on to an entirely different technique, so beware. It would be wise to test the opponent out by pretending to move in as he lifts his knee to see if it is a 'drawing' ploy.

LAY BACK;
Another seemingly simple defence that holds below its simplistic shell a demand for good distancing, timing and courage, for again you will be moving forward at a fast rate to employ your chosen counter attack.

As the opponent's front kick comes towards you move backwards and out of range by transferring your weight from the lead left leg to the rear right leg, bending the back leg enough to take you out of the kicks range. If this isn't enough you may slide back by moving your right leg a step backwards, followed by your left. Do not move so far back that you are out of range to employ a counter attack.

COUNTER ATTACKS;
As the kick is being retracted move quickly forward and counter attack with any punch, preferably a right cross or hook (body or head). Again, be careful that the front kick is not a ploy/feign to draw you on to another technique.

If and when the opening in the opponent's guard allows throw a combination of punches to follow the initially chosen counter attack.

SPINNING BACK KICK (STRAIGHT);
Probably the most powerful of all kicking techniques, relegated, thankfully to the realms of the 'advanced'.

I only see two methods of defence worth pursuing, the 'lay back/step back' and the 'close down'. The former being the most recommended.

LAY BACK/STEP BACK;
This is the only 'safe' method of deploying this cripple shooting kick, As is formerly described the lay back entails laying back, just outside the range of the attack and moving in with your counter attack as the kick is being retracted.

CLOSE DOWN;
As described, foregoingly, the close down demands timing, distancing and courage (in bagfulls), his is especially so with the back kick which does not suffer mistakes gladly.

Timing is of the essence, as the kicker begins his initial turn, move smartly forward with your chosen technique, striking before they can extend. (see illus).

THE SIDE KICK;

This can be a dangerous kick if applied by the advanced kicker, generally the side kick is 'pushy' and not what I would deem as dangerous, certainly when dealing with the masses.

Where the defences are the same as those formerly described please refer back for a more detailed description.

GEDANBARI;

This block may be used successfully to divert the side kick, it should be used in a direct facsimile to blocking the front kick. Counter attack with any right hand punch when blocking with the left hand, any left hand punch when blocking with the right hand. Follow with a combination of punches if the opening allows.

SOTOBARI;

Used to divert the side kick in a direct facsimile to blocking the front kick. Counter attack with any right hand punch, when blocking with the left hand, any left hand punch when blocking with the right.

LAY BACK;

As formerly described, lay back out side of the kicks range, as the attacker retracts the kick move smartly in with your chosen counter attack, preferably with a right cross or hook, followed where applicable, with a combination of punches.

GUARD BLOCK;

If the opponent is not particularly powerful it is possible to absorb the side kick on your guard. As you take the force of the blow lean forward slightly to avoid being pushed backwards and out of countering range. Counter with any punch, preferably a right cross or hook, combinations, again if the opening allows.

CLOSE DOWN;

This may be used against all kicks, the side kick being no exception. Try to move in as early as possible, preferably in the 'knee lift' stage of the kick. Any counter attack may be employed, combinations if and when possible.

TURNING KICKS;
This encompasses round house, back round house, spinning back round house and crescent kicks.

I rarely make an effort to block these type of kick, preferring to absorb them on a tight guard then counter attack heavily as the kicker retracts his leg, with the exception of the spinning back round house which is often too powerful to absorb. 'Lay back', 'step back' or 'close down' are the recommended defences against this kick.

ROUND HOUSE KICK; (body)
The left and right round house kick may be absorbed the arms employing the aforementioned 'guard block'. Counter attack with a right cross or hook as the kick is retracting.

LEFT GUARD BLOCK;
As the left round house kick comes towards your body, keep your guard tight and turn it and your torso to your left, meeting and absorbing the oncoming kick on your arms. From this position counter attack immediately, as the kick is retracting, with a left hook. follow with a combination, if possible.

'Close down' and 'lay back/step back' defences may also be effectively used against the left round house kick.

RIGHT GUARD BLOCK;
As the right leg round house kick comes towards your body, keep your guard tight, turn it and your torso to your right meeting and absorbing the oncoming kick on your arms. From this position counter immediately with a right cross or hook as the opponent retracts the kick. Follow with a combination if the opening allows.

FACE ROUND HOUSE; (Front and rear leg)

Face height round house kicks may be blocked and evaded in exactly the same manner as the body round house kick utilising the 'guard block', left and right guard block', 'close down' and 'lay back/step back'. Counter attacks to these defences are dictated by the opening left in the opponent's guard when his chosen kick is employed. In addition to the these defences the face round house (front leg or back) may be blocked with a left or right 'Palm block'.

PALM BLOCK;

As the right leg round house comes towards your face, strike your right hand to your left, across the front of your face, blocking the kick with the palm of hand on the lower ankle of the opponent's attacking leg (back of the heel, if blocking a back round house). Counter attack with a left jab, hook or uppercut (body or head) followed by a combination, if applicable.

The left round house is blocked in the same manner, using the right hand to counter attack as opposed to the left.

The best method of practising the foregoing defences and counter attacks is to practice them in pre-set and restricted sparring, restricting one partner to the use of only hand techniques and the other partner to the use of only kicking techniques.

In time and with much practice you will learn to mix and intermingle the aforementioned defences and counters, possibly spawning some new ones of your own. For greater detail on kicking techniques please refer to *Real Kicking*.

CHAPTER FIFTEEN

'HANDS AGAINST THE GRAPPLER'

Whilst J. F. Gilby (world wrestling and western boxing) stated that 'a puncher will always beat a kicker' he also finished the statement by saying that 'a grappler will always beat a puncher', a reckoning, Mr Gilby explains, derived from his empirical survey of fighters and fighting systems from all around the world. Again, in the main, I feel compelled to agree with him, though I fear that his statement does rely up on contributing factors.

When talking about the grappler beating the puncher (or kicker) it is fair to say that we are not just talking about some one who 'likes a bit of a wrestle' we are talking about a 'blood and snot' grappler who understands enough about the mechanics of punching to manipulate the pugilist's weaknesses, we are also presuming that the puncher has so little understanding of grappling that he will automatically lose if enters the wrestlers arena. If he hasn't any wrestling knowledge, he should have, or he should expect to lose, because a veteran grappler will be prepared to 'take a few' to gain grappling distance.

Whilst this is out of the purlieus of this text it is some thing we all should think about.

It is true that the grappler is the most dangerous of all adversaries, but he also has weaknesses that the pugilist may engineer and manipulate.

The key to fighting this omnipotent warrior is not to allow him a 'grip', once you do (if you do) you'll be at his mercy. Grappling range is quite unique. With kicking and punching range you can come in and out of it at will, once in grappling range you are usually there until the culmination of the fight.

As detailed in Chapter 17. Footwork. and in the 'restricted sparring' section of Chapter 13. Hand sparring, footwork is an imperative part of the fighting jigsaw, this is even more so when facing the grappler if a safe distance is to be kept between you and he.

Also, long range punches should be employed to keep the grappler at bay, more specifically the 'straight' long range punches. 'Hit and move' is the order of the day if grappling distance is to be avoided.

If your opponent does get closer to you than is desired short range uppercuts and hooks should be introduced, again with the onus up on hitting and moving.

Try not to move backwards, move to the side and around, clock wise and anti clock wise, though not too often in the same direction, if you do the grappler will be able to predict your movements and 'close you down'.

Grapplers do not, traditionally practise punching techniques, this reflects in their half mast and open 'guard' deeming them easy targets for the puncher, they are, however, notoriously tough, well used to pain and more than willing to take a few punches from you to bridge the gap, believing that they will 'win when in'.

Combinations should be kept to a minimum, 2, 3, 4 punches at the very most, a larger combination will see you rooted to one spot for too long, enough for the grappler to get a grip.

Uppercuts are prime punches for attacking the grappler who gets too close, punched underneath his arm/s as he stretches them out to get a grip on your attire, again, hit and move.

The gap between you and your wrestling adversary should, for your own safety, never shorten. Due to the fact that the grappler is seeking grappling range, he will be constantly moving forwards and towards you, his techniques can not be utilised until he gets a 'grip'. When he does move towards you strike out at him and then move away, do so for the duration of the fight. It is also good form to punch, if and when possible, at the grapplers fingers, if you can break them he can't use them.

Don't be disheartened if the adversary does not acknowledge or appear to weaken at or to your blows, good fighters discipline themselves not to show any signs of weakness or pain, this is a psychological tactic aimed at disheartening the weaker willed opponent (I do it all the time). Common sense will tell you that no man can take sever blows for ever, work away at your adversary like a corrosive, eventually he will erode.

The grapplers greatest asset out side of grappling range (probably his only asset) is 'intimidation'. He will just keep on coming, trying to wear down your stamina, and consequently your 'will', once that is beaten, so are you.

Restricted sparring with a partner is the best method of practising these methods. One partner is restricted to only punching techniques whilst the other is restricted to only grappling.

Start off lightly, build up until you are going 'all out' with the grappler doing every thing with in his power to grab you and you doing every thing within your power to stop him (both inside the bounds of the enforced restrictions).

Regular practice of the forgoing will enlighten the puncher to the enormity of the task before him, practice makes perfect.

When practising restricted sparring, as formerly described, the puncher should wear 16 oz boxing gloves for safety.

Although it is not within the realms of this text I would suggest to the reader that he acquire a basic knowledge of grappling techniques, just in case (or read my book *Real Grappling*).

CHAPTER SIXTEEN

CHEEKY SHOTS

If I have a forte the 'cheeky shot' is it. You may wish to label it differently, 'cheap shot' perhaps, the tag matters not, as long as they are effective, which they are.

The cheeky shot is hitting the opponent when he isn't ready or when his attention is or has been diverted.

Whilst in the dojo you may see these tactics as a little 'ungentlemanly', on the 'pavement arena' they are the norm, many battles are won and lost on the strengths and weaknesses of the 'cheeky shot'.

In this chapter I shall list my own favourites, but, be sure there are many more just waiting to be invented by the ingenious fighter who wants or needs an edge.

Samuri, great boxers, war mongers and gangsters through out history used the cheeky shot syndrome to fool their foe and bring them to defeat, as modern day gladiators, martial artists, pugilists or just 'bloody' fighters, I do not see why we should be any different.

The following techniques may be used in the dojo/gym or adapted to the 'street'.

EYE DISTRACTION;
Part way through the fight, slightly lower your guard and stare, left or right, behind your opponent as though distracted by some body (this works especially well if you are the instructor). More often than not your opponent will drop his own guard and follow your gaze. When he does, hit him (cheeky, hey ?) see illus.

TIRED PLOY;

Pretend to be tired by feigning exhaustion, whilst the opponent's attention is drawn to your dilemma (supposed) hit him.

LEG SLAP;

Mid way through the fight slap your left lead leg with your left hand, bounce from the slap, which will momentarily distract the opponent, in to a sharp left jab.

FINGER POINTING TO THE MOON;

From your guard position lift your left lead hand (or right if you wish to attack with the right hand) high and to your left. As soon as the opponent's eyes focus on the hand whip it in to a left jab (right cross, if using the right hand) directed in to the opponent's face (see illus).

SLOW STEP;
Mid way through the fight suddenly drop your guard and relax, step to your left, left leg crossing right (right crossing left if you wish to move the opposite way). Mid way through the step, as the legs cross, lash out with a fast left jab (right cross, if attacking with the right hand, moving to your right). This often catches the opponent 'clean' because he doesn't expect you to attack whilst you are stepping.

INSTEP ADJUSTMENT;
Momentarily stop sparring to adjust or straighten your 'gi' (Karate uniform) or shin protectors. As you bend to do so and the opponent's eyes follow your decent, quickly lash out with a jab or a cross.

In Dojo sparring I use the foregoing ploys as a bit of fun, paradoxically, I have also used them in 'live' scenarios when 'fun' was not on the agenda. If perfected they can mean the difference between winning and losing.

CHAPTER SEVENTEEN

THE DOUBLE HIP

BY PETER CONSTERDINE 7th DAN

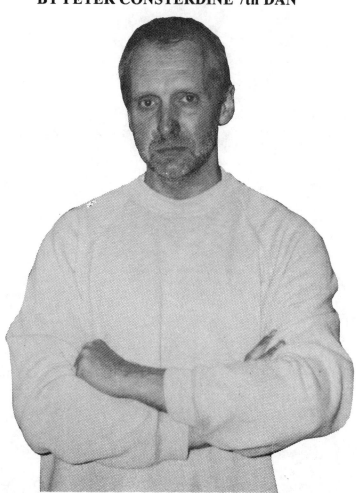

It was probably some four years or so after starting Karate that I actually learned how to punch with power. The revelation came, and I can only describe it as that, when I changed styles and took up Shukokai Karate. The Shukokai we practised then was really the product of one man, Shigeru Kimura Sensei, a Japanese who was not constrained mentally from questioning the effectiveness of traditional teaching.

By studying other sports and with the appliance of physics he had developed a basis of movement, speed, explosiveness and power in punches and kicks that can only be described as awesome. Although he was eventually to alter the techniques, for me the peak of power I was able to obtain was never better than that derived from these original techniques.

The main technique was, for me, the 'Double Hip'. It is this movement with its whipping action similar to throwing rather than punching that gives a technique its power. Every Karate man, Boxer, or Martial Artist who punches is taught to turn their hip into the punch, but unfortunately at the same time as the hand and this is where the problem arises. Also they are taught to pull back with the opposite side of the body, effectively rotating the body around a central pivot going through the head and out the backside.

In simple physics terms this means that if the axis is fixed the pullback gives as much power going backwards as it does to the punch going forwards. Try throwing a stone and keep the arm and hip together with no split between the two - it wouldn't reach the end of a small room! What in fact happens when you throw something is that the hip is whipped backwards and then forwards whilst leaving the arm behind to recoil, this recoil occurring in the shoulder. This split between the hip and arm with the double action is the first part of the double hip technique for punching. What also has to happen is that the pivot point must change from the central axis centred through the body to a 'door hinge' at the point of the leading hip. When the double hip occurs it must also involve a movement of body weight with the centre of balance shifting from between the two feet to being over the lead leg. The lead hip is then the pivot around which the body weight travels forward whipping that weight through the recoil in the shoulder and eventually through the arm.

The object is, in as natural a way as possible, to put all the body weight at the end of the fist and whilst it seems complicated the action is a very natural one and one that we would instinctively incline to if we had to project a heavy object ballistically. You'll see the same action in a shotput, javelin, tennis serve and golf stroke.

Relaxation is the key to success as any degree of tension restricts the recoil at the shoulder point and makes the double hip movement too mechanical losing the necessary flow. The success of the technique in a Self Defence role is that tremendous impact can be delivered at close ranges, particularly to the body, and most importantly from a variety of relaxed hand positions. It isn't necessary to raise the hands to punch and often, in fact, it is stronger when a punch is delivered from belt level as distinct from shoulder level due to the relaxed nature of the arm. At all times the arm must piston alongside the ribs with no lateral elbow movement to shed power or telegraph the punch.

The back leg must be allowed to come forward. The stance you should be in would be relaxed and again non-threatening and this assists the power as it prevents the rear leg being too stiff and rooted to the ground. Often a long traditional stance is a hindrance to delivering power as mistakenly the rear leg is held in its position and by doing so restricts the movement of the hips and body weight going forward. The power of the punch is actually derived from the pulling action of the front leg and not any pushing from the rear. Power for both punching and kicking is contained within the body's mid-section, but generations of punchers have mentally deceived themselves that the arms and shoulders are where the power is generated. These are simply transmission points through which the body's main power, its weight, is transmitted and that transmission is derived from the fast whipping action of the double hip around the lead hip door hinge. Few people would be able to withstand the impact from a correctly delivered body shot and the same technique with a faster hand action and shortened hip is equally as effective on the jawline.

It is impossible to obtain the true feeling from the text or photographs as to the power developed over such distances, but hopefully you should derive some impression as to the impact produced.

CHAPTER EIGHTEEN

TRAINING EQUIPMENT

Punching, as with all forms of combat, is an apprenticeship. As with all apprenticeships 'tools' are needed to enhance and sharpen the sought after skill. The 'tools' that I recommend for 'hand' training are as follows;

FOCUS PADS (HOOK AND JAB) ;

Potentate amongst training aids are the focus pads. Excellent for the development of accuracy, power, distancing and multi angled punching.

Each pad is centred by a 1+'' (diam) spot that acts as the target area. Any thing but a direct hit on the spot will look, feel and sound wrong. An accurate shot will feel solid and emit a definite 'thwack' letting you know that you are on target.

The focus pads are excellent for any one wishing to develop a K.O. punch.

It is necessary to have a partner when practising the pads. He should put one pad on each hand and turn them to meet the angle of your desired punch.

Spot facing inwards for hook punches, downwards for uppercuts and forwards for straight punches.

The person punching the pads should lead with his left leg (right if south paw) punching the pads with his left hand to his partners left hand, and his right hand to his partners right. The puncher should employ a guard in normal practice, no guard in 'line up' practice.

The holder should vary the height and distance (from the puncher) of the pads to promote variety.

As the puncher hits the pads he should exhale through his nose or mouth, this will regulate the breathing, feed the working muscles with oxygen and assist 'Kime' (body focus).

Once the puncher becomes familiar with hitting the pads and the holder with holding them correctly, the holder may dictate and control the play by shouting out punches or combinations of punches for the puncher to execute, 'jab, cross' 'right hook, left hook' etc. then change the angle of the pads to receive the designated strikes.

The experienced puncher may attempt more advanced combinations, again the holder must move the pads in time with the strikes.

The holder should not stay in the same position all of the time, he should move forcing the puncher to utilise good footwork. Each time the puncher finishes his attack upon the pads the holder should move to a different position.

TOP AND BOTTOM BALL;
Suspended in mid air, via a length of elastic from the ceiling to the floor (some times called the 'floor to ceiling ball') the top and bottom emerges as a wonderful training implement that is excellent for the development of timing and distancing. Some argue that the top and bottom is the closest one can get to a 'live' opponent. I am not inclined to disagree. It is also a hugely enjoyable method of practice.

It may be used to practice jabs, crosses, hooks and, to the advanced player, uppercuts. A very versatile training aid. The height (and thus speed) of the ball can be altered by tightening or loosening the straps above and below the ball.

In practice, after you have hit the ball, it will, if you are not vigilant, hit you back on its return or 'bounce back'. This adds to the realism of the practice immeasurably.

THE PUNCH BAG;
Probably the oldest method of practice known to fighting man. Despite its ancient heritage it is still the finest power developing instrument on the market. Also known to be excellent for the

development of good technique, stamina and combination punching. Due to the mass of the punch bag accuracy development is not greatly evolved here, though every thing else is.

The greatest form of practice, without a doubt, is to be had with the 'live' partner (dead ones just don't respond the same) with whom you can communicate, learn and progress.

When working with a partner, tell each other when a technique feels right, wrong, realistic, unrealistic, powerful, weak etc. etc. To talk to each other is to learn from each other.

EPILOGUE

When the time comes and you find your self facing a confrontational situation, punching will be the most immediate, accessible and effective tool that is naturally available to you.

Having faced over 300 opponents in 'live' situations, believe me, I know. Not either because I cannot or do not kick/grapple, I can (and occasionally do) kicking distance in the street scenario is rarer than elephant eggs.

Good hand techniques can and will neutralise/destroy an adversary quickly and clinically. Excellent 'hands' will safely vehicle you through any environment in any country of the world, safe in the knowledge that you are protected. Protected by something that you carry with you everywhere, that is legal in any environment, and that also has a thousand other uses besides 'protection'.

THE BRITISH COMBAT ASSOCIATION
THE ONLY ASSOCIATION DEDICATED TO SELF DEFENCE

Two of Britain's foremost Self Defence Instructors, Geoff Thompson and Peter Consterdine, have joined forces to form an Association which will promote the activities of Martial Artists pursuing the more practical aspects of their systems.

If you teach predominantly Self Defence or practical Martial Arts, then consider the following:

- *Are you fed up with the politics of large Association?*
- *Are you fully supported by the traditional groups?*
- *Are you prevented from seeking a wider range of instruction?*
- *Do you find it difficult to make your views felt? Is getting publicity for your group difficult?*
- *Are you and your junior instructors covered for liability insurance?*

- *Do you lack a regular flow of information on practical Martial Arts?*
- *Would you like to become a recognised Self Protection Instructor on a prestigious Register?*
- *Do you need assistance in promoting your Self Protection Course?*
- *Are you looking for Bodyguard and Small Arms Training?*

In the **British Combat Association**, together with its associated **Combat School and Self Protection Register**, we feel we have the answers. We can provide recognition, regular specialist training, gradings, insurance cover and a forum for your views. Your Club or Group will be actively promoted and publicised and the Association will, through a comprehensive syllabus and instructor assessment, professionalise the teaching of Self Protection.

The Register of Self Protection Instructors will become the prestigious reference point for people seeking professional teachers of Self Defence.

For an information pack
send a large SAE to:-

The British Combat Association
Chel Centre
26 Roundhay Road
Leeds
LS7 1AB

Tel: 0532 429686 (Daytime office) or
Geoff Thompson on 0203 361741 or
Peter Consterdine on 0831 576509

In association with:-
The British Combat School & The Association & Register of Self Protection Instructor

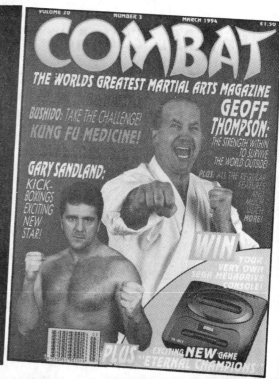

CENTRAL ENGLAND   KARATE ASSOCIATION

KARATE

COMPETITION KARATE

THE PAVEMENT ARENA

CHIEF INSTRUCTORS.
IAN McCRANOR (FOUNDER)
GEOFF THOMPSON

TRADITIONAL KARATE

EKGB

- **.Squad Training**
- **.Trips Abroad**
- **.Regional Courses etc**

CENTRAL ENGLAND KARATE ASSOCIATION

FOR INSTRUCTORS INFORMATION
CONTACT ➡

19 Glebe Farm Grove, Bridgeacre Gardens, Sprin
Valley, Coventry, CV3 2NE. Telephone: (0203) 443